Boko Haram Emerging Threat to the U.S. Homeland: December 1, 2011

U.S. Government Printing Office

112TH CONGRESS *1st Session* }	COMMITTEE PRINT	{ COMMITTEE PRINT 112–B

BOKO HARAM
Emerging Threat to the U.S. Homeland

SUBCOMMITTEE ON
COUNTERTERRORISM AND INTELLIGENCE
COMMITTEE ON HOMELAND SECURITY
HOUSE OF REPRESENTATIVES

December 2011

FIRST SESSION

U.S. GOVERNMENT PRINTING OFFICE

71–725 PDF   WASHINGTON : 2011

COMMITTEE ON HOMELAND SECURITY

PETER T. KING, New York, *Chairman*

LAMAR SMITH, Texas
DANIEL E. LUNGREN, California
MIKE ROGERS, Alabama
MICHAEL T. McCAUL, Texas
GUS M. BILIRAKIS, Florida
PAUL C. BROUN, Georgia
CANDICE S. MILLER, Michigan
TIM WALBERG, Michigan
CHIP CRAVAACK, Minnesota
JOE WALSH, Illinois
PATRICK MEEHAN, Pennsylvania
BEN QUAYLE, Arizona
SCOTT RIGELL, Virginia
BILLY LONG, Missouri
JEFF DUNCAN, South Carolina
TOM MARINO, Pennsylvania
BLAKE FARENTHOLD, Texas
MO BROOKS, Alabama

BENNIE G. THOMPSON, Mississippi
LORETTA SANCHEZ, California
SHEILA JACKSON LEE, Texas
HENRY CUELLAR, Texas
YVETTE D. CLARKE, New York
LAURA RICHARDSON, California
DANNY K. DAVIS, Illinois
BRIAN HIGGINS, New York
JACKIE SPEIER, California
CEDRIC L. RICHMOND, Louisiana
HANSEN CLARKE, Michigan
WILLIAM R. KEATING, Massachusetts
KATHLEEN C. HOCHUL, New York
VACANCY

MICHAEL J. RUSSELL, *Staff Director & Chief Counsel*
KERRY ANN WATKINS, *Senior Policy Director*
MICHAEL S. TWINCHEK, *Chief Clerk*
I. LANIER AVANT, *Minority Staff Director*

CONTENTS

BOKO HARAM

EMERGING THREAT TO THE U.S. HOMELAND

I. INTRODUCTION

On August 26, 2011, a suicide bomber drove a vehicle-borne improvised explosive device (VBIED) into the United Nations (U.N.) headquarters in Abuja, Nigeria, killing 23 people and injuring more than 80 others.[1] Responsibility for the bombing, one of the deadliest in the United Nations' history, was claimed by Boko Haram, an Islamist religious sect turned insurgent group based in the predominantly Muslim northern Nigeria. While this attack occurred inside Nigerian borders, it was the first time Boko Haram had targeted an international, non-Nigerian entity.

The attack marked a significant shift in the targeting and goals of the group, largely unknown to the U.S. Intelligence Community, and capped off an evolution in the capabilities of Boko Haram, beginning in the mid-2000s, from attacks with poisoned arrows and machetes to sophisticated car bombings.[2] In a video that surfaced in Nigeria in the weeks following the U.N. bombing, the perpetrator of the attack described the United Nations as a forum for "all global evil" and stated the attacks were designed to "send a message to the U.S. President and 'other infidels.'"[3]

According to Ambassador Anthony Holmes, Deputy to the Commander for Civil-Military Activities (DCMA) of United States Africa Command (AFRICOM), members of Boko Haram are being trained by Al Qaeda in the Lands of the Islamic Maghreb (AQIM).[4] They are also believed to have ties to the Somalian militant group al Shabaab.[5] This cooperation, combined with the increased sophistication of attacks executed by Boko Haram, have led to concerns from the U.S. Intelligence Community over the sect's intent and capability to strike Western targets in Nigeria, throughout Africa, and most importantly, the U.S. homeland.

Historically, Boko Haram has been focused on Nigerian government targets. Until recently, Western intelligence services did not widely view Boko Haram as a potential threat. Even after the U.N. attack, Nigerian experts remain skeptical about Boko Haram's intent and capability to strike U.S. interests and the homeland.

However, in the recent past, the U.S. Intelligence Community has underestimated the intent and capability of other terrorist groups to launch attacks against the U.S. homeland. The most notable recent examples include al Qaeda in the Arabian Peninsula (AQAP), and Tehrik-i-Taliban Pakistan (TTP), also known as the

---

[1] "Nigeria UN bomb: Video of 'Boko Haram' bomber released," BBC News, September 18, 2011. Available at: *http://www.bbc.co.uk/news/world-africa-14964554.*
[2] "Islamist attacks in Nigeria: A taste of the Taliban," *The Economist*, July 31, 2009. Available at: *http://www.economist.com/node/14156107?story_id=14156107.*
[3] BBC News, supra note 1.
[4] Al Qaeda-linked group finds fertile territory in Nigeria as killings escalate," Paul Cruickshank and Tom Lister, CNN, November 18, 2011, pg. 2. Available at: *http://articles.cnn.com/2011-11-18/africa/world_africa_nigeria-militants_1_boko-haram-maiduguri-nigerian-state/2?_s=PM:AFRICA.*
[5] Ibid., 3.

Pakistani Taliban. The U.S. Intelligence Community and outside counterterrorism and intelligence experts assessed that AQAP and TTP were regionally-based groups with a target set limited to Western supported governments or, at worst, American interests in the Middle East and South Asia. These assessments and general assumptions nearly proved fatal when a series of attempted attacks planned, directed, and executed by these two groups were thwarted on Christmas Day 2009 on Northwest Airlines Flight 253 over Detroit, and in May 2010 in New York City's Times Square. Given the ability of these other groups to become operational with apparently meager resources, it would be prudent for the U.S. Government to thoroughly and carefully examine the extent of the threat from Boko Haram to the U.S. homeland.

As Chairman and Ranking Member of the U.S. House of Representatives Committee on Homeland Security Subcommittee on Counterterrorism and Intelligence, it is our duty to examine all threats to the U.S. homeland. Boko Haram's recent escalation has prompted us to examine the group's potential, intent, and capability to attack United States interests and the U.S. homeland. This report will discuss the evolution of Boko Haram, its goals, and potential to commit acts of terrorism against U.S. interests and the U.S. homeland. This report will further discuss Nigerian counterterrorism capabilities, current U.S. diplomatic efforts, and future U.S. engagement and assistance options to assist the Nigerian government in countering the threat posed by Boko Haram. It is our hope that the conclusions in this report will raise awareness about the emerging threat posed by Boko Haram.

This report is based on open source information and extensive unclassified briefings from Government and non-Government entities. However, it should be noted that because of the speed with which Boko Haram has evolved as a terrorist group, little is known about the sect. Information is murky and academic research is limited. This report attempts to shed light on Boko Haram and the emerging threat it poses to U.S. interests and the homeland. To the extent this report spurs additional scholarship and intelligence collection, the U.S. Government will benefit and the American people will be safer.

Patrick Meehan
Chairman

Jackie Speier
Ranking Member

II. FINDINGS

1. Boko Haram has quickly evolved and poses an emerging threat to U.S. interests and the U.S. homeland.
2. Boko Haram has the intent and may be developing capability to coordinate on a rhetorical and operational level with al Qaeda in the Lands of the Islamic Maghreb (AQIM) and al Shabaab.
3. Boko Haram's evolution in targeting and tactics closely tracks that of other al-Qaeda affiliates that have targeted the U.S. homeland, most notably Al Qaeda in the Arabian Peninsula (AQAP) and Tehrik-i-Taliban Pakistan (TTP).
4. The U.S. Intelligence Community largely underestimated the potential for al-Qaeda affiliate groups to target the U.S. homeland, wrongly assessing they had only regional ambitions and threats against the U.S. homeland were merely "aspirational."
5. The United States should work with the Government of Nigeria to build counterterrorism and intelligence capability to effectively counter Boko Haram.

III. RECOMMENDATIONS

1. *Do Not Underestimate Boko Haram's Intent and Capability to Attack the U.S. Homeland.*—As this report makes clear, the U.S. Intelligence Community has recently underestimated the intent and capability of terrorist groups to strike the homeland, most notably Al Qaeda in the Arabian Peninsula (AQAP) and Tehrik-i-Taliban Pakistan (TTP). These underestimations had near-deadly consequences on Christmas Day 2009 over Detroit and in May 2010 in Times Square.

3. *Determine Whether Boko Haram Should be Designated a Foreign Terrorist Organization (FTO).*—The Secretary of State should conduct an investigation into whether Boko Haram should be designated a Foreign Terrorist Organization, in accordance with Section 219 of the Immigration and Nationality Act (INA), as amended. Following the Boko Haram attack on the United Nations (U.N.) headquarters in Abuja, Nigeria, we wrote to Secretary of State Hillary Clinton calling for an investigation to determine whether FTO designation was necessary. In light of Boko Haram's continued escalation, FTO designation may be required to provide our intelligence and law enforcement communities the tools necessary to ensure Boko Haram does not attack U.S. interests and the U.S. homeland.

3. *Increase U.S. Intelligence Community Collection on Boko Haram.*—The U.S. Intelligence Community must increase its intelligence collection on Boko Haram, including human intelligence (HUMINT) and signals intelligence (SIGINT). It must also enhance its liaison relationship with Nigerian security services and help build their capacity to combat the threat posed by Boko Haram to Nigerian and U.S. interests.

4. *Conduct Outreach with Nigerian Diaspora Communities in the United States.*—The U.S. Government should develop relationships with Nigerian diaspora communities in the United States to learn more about Boko Haram and the factors driving its evolution, intent, capability, and targeting. Through familial and personal rela-

tionships, diaspora communities in the United States provide a unique and invaluable perspective on their home country.

5. *Increase U.S. Government Support for Nigerian Counterterrorism and Intelligence Programs.*—The U.S. Government should increase its support for programs that enhance the ability of Nigerian security forces to more effectively target Boko Haram and counter its evolution. The U.S. and Nigerian governments should also work more closely to increase intelligence collection.

IV. ORIGINS AND HISTORY

UPRISING

"Boko Haram," which in the local Hausa language means "Western education is forbidden," officially calls itself "Jama'atul Alhul Sunnah Lidda'wati wal Jihad," which means "people committed to the propagation of the Prophet's teachings and jihad."[6] Though the origins of Boko Haram are murky, the group was not founded as a violent insurgency bent on overthrowing the Nigerian government. Founded in the mid-1990s as a religious study group, Boko Haram did not begin to transform into the insurgent group it is today until a young and charismatic Nigerian civil service employee named Mohammed Yusuf assumed control. Calling themselves the Nigerian Taliban, Boko Haram adopted a "live-off-the-land" lifestyle and established a camp in a remote area of northeast Nigeria, which the group dubbed "Afghanistan."[7]

From 2002–2009, Boko Haram engaged in low-level conflict with local police forces and non-compliant villagers. In 2009, a crackdown on Boko Haram members from Nigerian police forces in Borno state erupted into fighting. On July 26, 2009, sect members launched an attack against a police station in Bauchi state, resulting in the death of 39 Boko Haram members, two police officers, and one soldier.[8] This ignited a 5-day stand-off between Boko Haram and security personnel that saw violent attacks and battles spread across four northern Nigerian states: Bauchi, Kano, and Yobe, culminating in a final battle in the city of Maiduguri in Borno state.

On July 30, 2009, the battle of Maiduguri ended when Nigerian security forces captured and killed Boko Haram's leader, Mohammed Yusuf, in what human rights groups have deemed an extrajudicial killing. Yusuf's execution was videotaped by soldiers and later broadcast on television.[9] In total, nearly 700 people were killed in the uprising. The death of Yusuf marked a turning point for the Boko Haram. It was forced underground and many of its leaders reportedly fled to other parts of Nigeria, including Bauchi state, as well as neighboring countries.[10]

RADICAL REEMERGENCE

In 2010, Boko Haram re-emerged radically more violent and determined to seek vengeance against the Nigerian state for executing its leader. Under the leadership of Imam Abubakar Shekau, who claimed to have assumed control of the sect following the death of Mohammed Yusuf, Boko Haram militants carried out violent operations against government targets in the north. The most notable include an assault on a Maiduguri prison that resulted in

---

[6] "Boko Haram," Toni Johnson, Council on Foreign Relations, November 7, 2011. Available at: *http://www.cfr.org/africa/boko-haram/p25739.*

[7] "Boko Haram: History, ideas, and revolt [2]." Shehu Sani, *The Guardian*, July 8, 2011. Available at: *http://www.guardiannewsngr.com/index.php?option=com_content&view=article&-id=53730:boko-haramhistory-ideas-and-revolt-2&catid=72:focus&Itemid=598.*

[8] "Boko Haram: History, ideas, and revolt [4]." Shehu Sani, *Vanguard*, July 8, 2011. Available at: *http://www.vanguardngr.com/2011/07/boko-haram-history-ideas-and-revolt-4/.*

[9] "Boko Haram: History, ideas, and revolt [5]." Shehu Sani, *Vanguard*, July 7, 2011. Available at: *http://www.vanguardngr.com/2011/07/boko-haram-history-ideas-and-revolt-5/.*

[10] "Nigeria Conflict Assessment," USAID, August 2011, pg. 39.

the release of 700 prisoners, including Boko Haram members, and a bombing in the city of Jos that killed more than 80 people. Significantly, the targeting of the Nigerian capital city of Abuja represented an evolving target set outside of Northern Nigeria. In June 2011, Boko Haram militants bombed the police headquarters in Abuja, and finally, carried out the suicide attack against the Abuja U.N. headquarters 2 months later.

A number of factors have been attributed to fueling Boko Haram's violence and fanaticism, including a feeling of alienation from the wealthier, Christian, oil-producing, southern Nigeria, pervasive poverty, rampant government corruption, heavy-handed security measures, and the belief that relations with the West are a corrupting influence. These grievances have led to sympathy among the local Muslim population despite Boko Haram's violent tactics.[11]

Residents in northern Nigeria live in extreme poverty. In Maiduguri, most residents live on less than $2 a day.[12] Shettima Khalifa Dikwa, chairman of the Voters Forum at the University of Maiduguri, blamed the government and heavy security practices for the growing public sympathy toward Boko Haram. "If it escalates it is the fault of the government and JTF (Joint Task Force). You can't have JTF searching your house, invading your privacy, mistreating people without you having sympathy for Boko Haram."[13] These grievances and the failure of the government to effectively address them serve as a key recruiting tool for Boko Haram.

Boko Haram's desire to rid northern Nigeria of these problems serves as the primary motives behind their stated ambition to implement Sharia Law and establish an Islamic state.[14] Sharia Law currently exists in 12 out of 36 Nigerian states as the result of a grassroots movement that coincided with Nigeria's transition to democracy in 1999.[15]

A consistent lack of reliable reporting on Boko Haram has contributed to the difficulty in assessing its size, makeup, and goals. Boko Haram operates out of Maiduguri, the capital city of Borno state in northeast Nigeria bordered by Chad, Cameroon, and Niger. The group's membership is elusive. Some describe the "core Boko Haram" as the immediate followers of the late sect leader Mohammed Yusuf. However, others consider Boko Haram to be more of a "grassroots insurrection," or an "amorphous cloud" that has emerged from the larger context of Muslim grievances and frustration with the government.

V. FROM "ASPIRATION" TO THE U.S. HOMELAND

Boko Haram's activities over the last 2 years mark an escalation in the frequency and violence of its attacks. On February 10, 2011, Director of National Intelligence (DNI) James Clapper delivered the Worldwide Threat Assessment of the U.S. Intelligence Community and stated that Boko Haram was "focused on local issues.

---

[11] "In Nigeria's northeast, some sympathy for Islamists," Joe Brock, *Reuters*, November 14, 2011. Available at: *http://in.reuters.com/article/2011/11/14/idINIndia-60515120111114*.
[12] Ibid.
[13] Ibid.
[14] Johnson, supra note 6.
[15] Ibid.

[and] may be pursuing interests it shares with AQIM."[16] Boko Haram's activities since then mark an escalation in the frequency and violence of its attacks and an emboldened Boko Haram should warrant enhanced scrutiny from the U.S. Intelligence Community.

In order to properly gauge the true threat Boko Haram will pose to U.S. interests and potentially the U.S. homeland in the future, it may be useful to examine two other groups whose rapid expansion in capabilities and apparent evolution in targeting and goals took the United States by surprise. Al Qaeda in the Arabian Peninsula (AQAP) and Tehrik-i-Taliban Pakistan (TTP), both newly formed groups, were viewed by the U.S. Intelligence Community and outside experts as regionally focused and content to launch strikes against their home governments and Western interests in the region. In both cases, the Intelligence Community—and the country—were caught off guard when attacks were launched by AQAP and TTP against the U.S. homeland. The rapid evolution of Boko Haram as a threat shares certain characteristics with AQAP and TTP; an examination of the rise of these two groups may be useful in projecting the future threat of Boko Haram.

AL QAEDA IN THE ARABIAN PENINSULA (AQAP)

In January 2009, the al-Qaeda branches in Saudi Arabia and Yemen merged into Al Qaeda in the Arabian Peninsula.[17] The creation of AQAP concerned U.S. intelligence officials, but the widely-held assessment was that AQAP intended to target the Saudi Arabian monarchy, the Yemeni government, and U.S. interests in the Gulf region. Twice in the months prior to the merger that created AQAP, the U.S. Embassy in Sana'a was attacked. Still, the U.S. Intelligence Community did not assess there was serious intent nor capability to launch attacks on American soil.

In August 2009, a suicide bomber detonated an explosive device hidden inside his body in an attempt to assassinate the Saudi Arabian Assistant Interior Minister Muhammad bin Nayef. It was a brazen plot that came close to killing a top U.S. terrorism ally, and represented AQAP's boldest terrorist attempt since the merger. It also signaled a quick evolution in sophistication of targeting and bomb-making.

On November 5, 2009, U.S. Army Major Nidal Malik Hasan opened fire on fellow soldiers at the Fort Hood Army base in Texas, killing 13 and wounding more than 30.[18] In the subsequent investigation, it was revealed that before the attack, Major Hasan corresponded via email with the future operational leader of AQAP, American-born cleric Anwar al-Awlaki.[19] Major Hasan's contact

---

[16] "Statement for the Record on the Worldwide Threat Assessment for the U.S. Intelligence Community," James R. Clapper, Director of National Intelligence, February 10, 2011, pg. 18. Available at: *http://www.dni.gov/testimonies/20110210_testimony_clapper.pdf.*

[17] "Al-Qa'ida in the Arabian Peninsula," National Counterterrorism Center website. Available at: *http://www.nctc.gov/site/groups/aqap.html.*

[18] "Fort Hood Suspect Yells Nidal Hasan's Name in Court," Pierre Thomas, Martha Raddatz, Rhonda Sewartz, Jason Ryan, ABC News, July 29, 2011. Available at: *http://abcnews.go.com/Blotter/fort-hoodsuspect-nabbed-al-qaeda-inspire-magazine/story?id=14187568#.TtS7YLJFuso.*

[19] Ibid. Anwar al-Awlaki was an American-born Muslim cleric of Yemeni descent. He was an imam at mosques in San Diego, CA and Falls Church, VA where it was suspected that he had ties to three of the 9/11 hijackers. After 9/11, he denounced the attacks and emerged as a voice of moderation within the Muslim community. This changed in 2002 when he left the United

Continued

with al-Awlaki served as an inspiration for the Fort Hood terrorist attack. This became the first incident in which an AQAP and al-Awlaki inspired attack took place on U.S. soil.

A little over 1 month later, on Christmas Day 2009, Umar Farouk Abdulmutallab, a Nigerian Muslim and the son of a prominent Nigerian government official, attempted to detonate a bomb on Northwest Airlines Flight 253 destined for Detroit. As the Airbus A330 with 289 people on board approached Detroit, Abdulmutallab attempted to detonate a bomb hidden in his underwear. When he failed to successfully detonate the explosive, passengers and flight crew quickly subdued him.[20] AQAP quickly claimed responsibility for the attack and promised that more attacks would follow.[21]

Similar to the Fort Hood case, the subsequent investigation revealed that Abdulmutallab had direct ties to AQAP, travelling to Yemen for instruction and deployment at a terrorist training camp.[22] The attack caught the U.S. Intelligence Community off guard as they did not believe AQAP had neither the intent nor capability to deploy militants to the United States to strike the U.S. homeland. During a press conference following the Flight 253 bombing attempt, John O. Brennan, Assistant to the President for Homeland Security and Counterterrorism stated: "The fact that they [AQAP] had moved forward to try to execute this attack against the homeland I think demonstrated to us—and this is what the review sort of uncovered—that we had a strategic sense of sort of where they were going, but we didn't know they had progressed to the point of actually launching individuals here."[23]

When Mr. Brennan was asked when it had become known that AQAP intended to attack the United States, he explained:

> "In the intelligence that we have acquired, over the past several years it's been rather aspirational. It has said things, it has promoted a certain view as far as bringing the fight to us, but all of their activities, at least that we were focused on, were happening in Yemen. They carried attacks against Prince Mohammed bin Nayef in Saudi Arabia, against Saudi targets, inside of Yemen, against Yemeni as well as against U.S. targets. So it was aspirational. We saw that there was this mounting sort of drumbeat of interest in trying to get individuals to carry out attacks. That was the fragmentary information.

States for London and eventually Yemen, where he became a proponent of militant Islam and encouraged attacks against Americans. He came to be viewed by many in the U.S. Intelligence Community as a greater threat to the United States than Osama bin Laden. On September 30, 2011, al-Awlaki was killed by a CIA drone strike in Yemen, after a 2-year manhunt.

[20] "The Radicalization of Umar Farouk Abdulmutallab." Mark Hosenball, *Newsweek*, January 1, 2010. Available at: *http://www.thedailybeast.com/newsweek/2010/01/01/the-radicalization-of-umar-faroukabdulmutallab.html.*

[21] "Al-Qaeda link investigated as clues emerge in foiled terror attack," CNN, December 28, 2009, pg. 2. Available at: *http://articles.cnn.com/2009-12-28/justice/airline.terror.attempt_1_al-qaeda-explosive-deviceyemeni/2?_s=PM:CRIME.*

[22] "Underwear Bomber: New video of Training, Martyrdom Statements," Matthew Cole, Brian Ross, and Nasser Atta, April 26, 2010. Available at: *http://abcnews.go.com/Blotter/underwear-bomber-videotraining-martyrdom-statements/story?id=10479470#.TtS9K7JFuso.*

[23] "Press Briefing by Napolitano, Brennan, and Gibbs on the attempted December 25, 2009 terrorist attack," Council on Foreign Relations, January 7, 2010. Available at: *http://www.cfr.org/terrorism/pressbriefing-napolitano-brennan-gibbs-december-25-2009-attempted-terrorist-attack/p21154.*

"And so in hindsight now—and 20/20 hindsight always gives you much better opportunity to see it—we saw the plot was developing, but at the time we did not know in fact that they were talking about sending Mr. Abdulmutallab to the United States.

"Now, remember, Mr. Abdulmutallab was a much different story in terms of a Nigerian who traveled to Yemen and then came over here. But what it clearly indicates is that there is a seriousness of purpose on the part of al Qaeda in the Arabian Peninsula to carry out attacks here in the United States—whether they're reaching people through the Internet, or whether or not, in fact, they are sending people abroad."[24]

On January 19, 2010, 3 weeks after the Christmas Day attempted attack, the Department of State officially declared AQAP as a foreign terrorist organization (FTO).[25]

Tehrik-i-Taliban Pakistan (TTP)

Tehrik-i-Taliban Pakistan, more commonly referred to as TTP or the Pakistani Taliban, was formed in 2007 as an alliance of militant groups dedicated to waging jihad against the Pakistani military and government and fighting to expel U.S. and NATO forces from Afghanistan.[26] They carried out numerous large-scale attacks in Afghanistan and Pakistan, and are reportedly tied to the assassination of former Prime Minister Benazir Bhutto in December 2007.[27] The TTP actively targets U.S. interests in Pakistan, including NATO supply lines, and has conducted multiple assaults on the U.S. consulate in Peshawar, among other American targets.

Despite their aggressive targeting of U.S. and NATO troops and facilities, the U.S. Intelligence Community assessed that TTP was a regional—and not a homeland—threat. [28] While the evolution of tactics by TTP did evoke concern among U.S. counterterrorism officials, the notion that the TTP would strike the homeland was dismissed by the Federal Bureau of Investigation (FBI). Even after TTP leader Baitullah Mehsud made threats against the White House in 2009, the FBI said in an emailed statement:

"The FBI is aware of the claims made by Baitullah Mehsud. He has made similar threats to the U.S. in the past and we deem these new statements as aspirational . . . ."[29]

On May 5, 2009, the State Department Special Representative for Afghanistan and Pakistan, the late Ambassador Richard

---

[24] Ibid.

[25] "Designations of Al-Qa'ida in the Arabian Peninsula (AQAP) and Senior Leaders," Philip J. Crowley, U.S. Department of State Press Release, January 19, 2010.

[26] "Tehrik-e Taliban Pakistan (TTP)." National Counterterrorism Center profile. Available at: *http://www.nctc.gov/site/groups/ttp.html.*

[27] Ibid.

[28] See footnotes 29 and 30. "The Taliban's Threats," and "From Strategy to Implementation: The Future of the U.S.-Pakistan Relationship." Available at: Available at: *http://foreignaffairs.house.gov/111/49547.pdf.*

[29] "The Taliban's Threats," Mark Hosenball, *The Daily Beast,* March 31, 2009. Available at: *http://www.thedailybeast.com/newsweek/2009/03/31/the-taliban-s-threats.html.*

Holbrooke, reiterated this belief in response to a question during testimony before the House Committee on Foreign Affairs:

> "In regard to al Qaeda, I think it is very well-described in an article in this morning's New York Times where a Taliban spokesman said we do the local war against the Americans, al Qaeda does the global war."[30]

On May 1, 2010, Faisal Shahzad, a Pakistan-born naturalized U.S. citizen, drove a 1993 Nissan Pathfinder 4x4 loaded with propane, gasoline, and fertilizer into New York City's Times Square.[31] Shahzad failed to successfully detonate the explosives before a street vendor alerted the New York Police Department (NYPD) about the abandoned, smoking vehicle. Following an intense manhunt by Federal, State, and local law enforcement agencies, Shahzad was caught 2 days later attempting to flee at John F. Kennedy International Airport onboard a departing flight to Dubai.

In the subsequent Federal investigation, it was discovered that Shahzad had purchased the car and explosive materials through funding provided to him by the TTP. He received a total of $12,000 in two separate cash payments through hawalas in Massachusetts and New York, which was sent from a TTP militant in Pakistan to carry out the attack. During questioning following his arrest, Shahzad confessed to traveling to Waziristan, Pakistan in December 2009 to receive explosives training from members of the TTP at a terrorist training camp, after which he received an additional $4,000.[32]

Notably, the State Department did not designate the TTP as a FTO until September 2010, 4 months after the attempted Times Square attack.[33] In summarizing the explanation given by an unnamed senior counterterrorism official as to why the TTP was not labeled a FTO sooner, *Newsweek* magazine wrote: "Until relatively recently, the TTP was thought to be targeting the Pakistani government exclusively—not the United States—and State Department officials were reluctant to intrude on what was largely regarded as an internal Pakistani problem."[34]

In the aftermath of the AQAP and TTP attempted attacks, the U.S. Intelligence Community admitted to underestimating the potential of these two groups to launch attacks against the homeland. The United States cannot afford to miscalculate Boko Haram's intent and capability to strike the homeland. The evolution of Boko Haram clearly illustrates it is a group with fast-growing ambitions. It is important for the U.S. Intelligence Community to stay ahead

---

[30] "From Strategy to Implementation: The Future of the U.S.-Pakistan Relationship," U.S. House of Representatives Committee on Foreign Affairs hearing, May 5, 2009.

[31] "Profile: Faisal Shahzad," BBC News, October 5, 2010. Available at: *http://www.bbc.co.uk/news/world-us-canada-11475789.*

[32] "Pakistani Taliban helped Faisal Shahzad, it's not on U.S. list of terrorists?" Liam Stack, *The Christian Science Monitor*, June 23, 2010. Available at: *http://www.csmonitor.com/World/terrorism-security/2010/0623/Pakistani-Taliban-helped-Faisal-Shahzad-it-s-not-on-US-list-of-terrorists.*

[33] "Pakistan Taliban given FTO designation," UPI.com Special Reports, September 2, 2010. Available at: *http://www.upi.com/Top_News/Special/2010/09/02/Pakistani-Taliban-given-FTO-designation/UPI-22681283446480/.*

[34] "U.S. Weighs Official 'Terrorist Organization' Status for the Pakistani Taliban," Michael Isikoff, *The Daily Beast, Newsweek*, May 11, 2010. Available at: *http://www.thedailybeast.com/newsweek/blogs/declassified/2010/05/11/u-s-weighs-official-terrorist-organization-status-for-the-pakistani-taliban.html.*

of Boko Haram in an effort to thwart a potential attack against the homeland.

VI. EVOLUTION AND COLLABORATION

Perhaps the most troubling aspect of the rise of Boko Haram in Nigeria is the reports of increasing collaboration between the group and al Qaeda in the Lands of the Islamic Maghreb (AQIM) and al Shabaab. The rapid evolution of Boko Haram may point to the sharing of weapons and expertise among various terrorist organizations across the African continent.

CHANGING TACTICS AND TARGETS: SUICIDE BOMBERS AND WESTERN TARGETS

There has been a significant shift in Boko Haram's targets, tactics, and geographic reach, particularly in the last year. The use of a suicide VBIED on the Abuja police barracks in June 2011 marked the first time on record a suicide attack was carried out in Nigeria. The bomb used was large enough to destroy 40 other vehicles in the parking lot, and it demonstrated the sect's ability to launch attacks outside of its traditional area of operations in the north, proving that they were now capable of targeting the capital.[35]

Boko Haram's traditional targets had been those affiliated with the Nigerian state. Past targets include police stations, army barracks, banks, churches, markets, teachers, and universities. Boko Haram has also attacked beer drinkers, card players, and those engaging in activities that they deem as un-Islamic.[36] The sect has also conducted targeted assassinations against religious and political leaders, particularly those individuals who have challenged or spoken out against the group or allied themselves with the government of Christian President Goodluck Jonathan. Before their recent bombing campaign, Boko Haram's signature tactic was drive-by shootings and bombings from motorbikes.[37]

The suicide attack launched against the U.N. headquarters in Abuja appears to be Boko Haram's first non-Nigerian, international target. The driver rammed the car into an exit gate and then drove into a parking garage before detonating the VBIED.[38] This is significant because " . . . the U.N. compound was located in the diplomatic district of Abuja, where numerous high-profile facilities are located, demonstrating that Boko Haram possessed the ability to spot a soft target amid harder targets like foreign embassies and government buildings."[39] The group also managed to successfully find and exploit the security gap at the exit gate. This indicates that some type of surveillance may have been conducted before the attack was launched.[40]

Some have described the attack on the U.N. headquarters as an attack driven against an entity that cooperates with the Nigerian

---

[35] "The Rising Threat from Nigeria's Boko Haram Militant Group," Scott Stewart, STRATFOR Global Intelligence, November 10, 2011. Available at: *http://www.stratfor.com/weekly/20111109-rising-threatnigerias-boko-haram-militant-group*.

[36] "The Rise of Boko Haram in Nigeria," David Cook, *CTC Sentinel*, September 2011, pg. 4.

[37] Ibid.

[38] Stewart, supra note 35.

[39] Ibid.

[40] Ibid.

government, and is by extension only targeting the Nigerian state. However, suicide attacks against Western targets working with the host government have in many instances marked the beginning of a new and advanced stage of insurgency. According to David Cook, writing for the West Point Combating Terrorism Center's *CTC Sentinel,* "While the attack on the police General Headquarters can be seen as a continuation of Boko Haram's fixation upon the Nigerian police and army, the United Nations attack is much more in line with other [global terrorist] organizations, and is strongly reminiscent of the suicide attack in Baghdad against the United Nations in August 2003, which was one of the opening blows of the Iraqi insurgency."[41]

COLLABORATION WITH AQIM AND AL SHABAAB

Boko Haram's evolving tactics and targeting may be the result of ties between AQIM in North Africa and al Shabaab in Somalia. Such cross-pollination of weapons, tactics, and bomb-making expertise can quickly increase the capabilities of terrorist groups, as seen in the Federally Administered Tribal Areas of Pakistan, and may have been a contributing factor to Boko Haram's advances. The Boko Haram leadership exile from Nigeria following the 2009 security forces crackdown may have also contributed. Members of Boko Haram appear to have connections in Niger, Chad, Cameroon, and Sudan, and it is believed that the sect has also purchased weapons in some of these countries.[42] These connections highlight the mobility and transnational nature of Boko Haram's operations.

Al-Qaeda militants operating in Nigeria is not unprecedented. In 2004, the Nigerian government charged Mohammed Ashafa, a Nigerian national claiming to be operating an al-Qaeda cell.[43] These charges included receiving money from al-Qaeda operatives in Pakistan for the purposes of recruiting and training terrorists to attack Americans in Nigeria.[44] In 2008, former police inspector-general, Mike Okiro, claimed that he had recovered evidence revealing a plot by bin Laden to conduct a bombing within Nigeria.[45] The rise of Boko Haram as a terrorist group in Nigeria may serve as a means by which al-Qaeda can infiltrate Nigeria. Moreover, a recent poll conducted by the Pew Research Center's Global Attitudes Projects on Muslim favorability toward bin Laden showed Nigerian Muslims as uniquely favorable to bin Laden and al-Qaeda. Throughout the past decade, Muslim populations have discredited bin Laden and al-Qaeda. However, unlike their counterparts elsewhere in the world, just under half—49 percent—of all Nigerian Muslims polled expressed more favorable views toward bin Laden and al-Qaeda in 2010.[46]

Over the past year, in response to successful counterterrorism crackdowns by North African governments, AQIM has reportedly

---

[41] Cook, supra note 36, at 5.
[42] USAID, supra note 10.
[43] "Bin Laden and Nigeria," Paul Ohia, *This Day Live,* May 3, 2011. Available at: *http://www.thisdaylive.com/articles/bin-laden-and-nigeria/90683/.*
[44] Ibid.
[45] Ibid.
[46] "Osama bin Laden Largely Discredited Among Muslim Publics in Recent Years," Pew Global Attitudes Project, May 2, 2011. Available at: *http://pewresearch.org/pubs/1977/poll-osama-bin-laden-death-confidence-muslim-publics-al-qaeda-favorability.*

been extending its operations into Mauritania, Mali, and Niger, among other places. Evidence has surfaced suggesting that AQIM is making a focused attempt to extend its area of operations and sphere of influence into the Sahel and sub-Saharan Africa. In August 2011, a video surfaced showing two Westerners who were kidnapped for ransom in Nigeria by AQIM. While kidnappings for ransom are not a new strategy for AQIM, extending their reach into Nigeria represents a marked expansion of geographic reach in kidnapping operations.[47]

As AQIM has moved south, it has reportedly become involved in drug trafficking and cultivated alliances with criminal organizations in the Sahel to expand its reach and enhance its operational capacity. According to Dr. J. Peter Pham, this strategy is, in effect, the "subcontracting" of operations to local militant groups.[48] As Mohammed Mokaddem, an Algerian journalist and author of a recent book about AQIM stated: "[AQIM] has never hidden its ambition to bring in the Islamists of Nigeria in particular at the very moment when sectarian strife and conflict between Muslims and Christians is on the rise."[49] U.S. intelligence officials have also suspected that AQIM operatives were extending their reach southward. Three years ago, in the 2008 Annual Threat Assessment from the U.S. Intelligence Community, AQIM's reach into Nigeria was clear: "AQIM traditionally has operated in Algeria and northern Mali and has recruited and trained an unknown, but probably small, number of extremists from Tunisia, Morocco, Nigeria, Mauritania, Libya, and other countries."[50]

African governments have been open about their concerns regarding Boko Haram and AQIM collaboration. In November 2011, the Algerian Deputy Foreign Minister, Abdelkader Messahel, issued a public warning that Algerian intelligence found evidence of cooperation between Boko Haram and AQIM. "We have no doubts that coordination exists between Boko Haram and al-Qaeda. The way both groups operate and intelligence reports show there is cooperation."[51] Algeria's public acknowledgement of cooperation between Boko Haram and AQIM is significant. Algeria currently serves as AQIM's base of operations and the Algerian government conducts the largest intelligence-gathering operation on AQIM of any country in Africa.[52]

Boko Haram has also been reportedly collaborating with al Shabaab, an al-Qaeda linked militant Islamist group in Somalia and a U.S. State Department designated FTO. It has been reported that some members of Boko Haram have trained in Somalia as al Shabaab has made an effort in recent years to recruit outsiders in both Africa and the United States. Despite being involved in a civil war, al Shabaab has launched attacks outside of Somalia, most no-

[47] "Al-Qaeda's North African Franchise Moves South," Dr. J. Peter Pham, The Atlantic Council, August 5, 2011. Available at: *http://www.acus.org/new__atlanticist/al-qaeda%E2%80%99s-north-african-franchise-moves-south*.
[48] Ibid.
[49] Ibid.
[50] "Annual Threat Assessment of the Intelligence Community for the Senate Armed Services Committee," J. Michael McConnell, Office of the Director of National Intelligence, February 27, 2008, pg. 6. Available at: *http://www.dni.gov/testimonies/20080227__testimony.pdf*.
[51] "Algeria says Nigeria's Boko Haram tied to al Qaeda," *Reuters*, MSNBC, November 13, 2011. Available at: *http://www.msnbc.msn.com/id/45277821/ns/world__news-africa/#*.
[52] Ibid.

tably twin suicide nightclub bombings during the World Cup in Kampala, Uganda on July 11, 2010.[53]

Skeptics of Boko Haram's ties to al Shabaab cite the fact that both groups are concerned mainly with their respective countries. Somalia and Nigeria are on opposite ends of the continent, making the long distance between them a hindrance to cooperation. However, members of Boko Haram's leadership have studied in Saudi Arabia and desire to build relationships with other extremists outside Nigeria. [54] Most importantly, however, Boko Haram has admitted to establishing links in Somalia. A statement allegedly released by the sect read, "Very soon, we will wage jihad . . . We want to make it known that our jihadists have arrived in Nigeria from Somalia where they received real training on warfare from our brethren who made that country ungovernable . . . This time round, our attacks will be fiercer and wider than they have been."[55]

A GENERAL'S WARNING

On August 17, 2011, U.S. Army General Carter F. Ham, Commander of AFRICOM called attention to Boko Haram's expanding ambitions, telling the *Associated Press* that intelligence indicated Boko Haram had made contact with operatives from both AQIM and al Shabaab:

> "What is most worrying at present is, at least in my view, a clearly stated intent by Boko Haram and by al Qaeda in the Islamic Maghreb to coordinate and synchronize their efforts. I'm not so sure they're able to do that just yet, but it's clear to me they have the desire and intent to do that."[56]

On June 14, 2010, AQIM leader Abu Musab Abd al-Wadoud, also known as Abdelmalik Droukdel, told *al-Jazeera* that his group would provide Boko Haram with weapons, support, and training.[57] Since those comments, there have been public reports that Boko Haram fighters have been seen training in AQIM camps.[58]

In August 2011, one week *before* the U.N. bombing in August, Nigerian authorities arrested two Boko Haram militants. The detainees, who were still in custody after the U.N. bombing, allegedly told Nigerian investigators that another Boko Haram member, Mamman Nur, had led the attack. Nur reportedly has links to al-Qaeda and had recently returned from Somalia.[59]

In September 2011, European Union Counterterrorism Coordinator Gilles de Kerchove warned of collaboration between the two groups: "There is still nothing structural. There are efforts at con-

---

[53] "Al-Shabaab," National Counterterrorism Center profile. Available at: *http://www.nctc.gov/site/groups/al_shabaab.html.*
[54] USAID, supra note 10.
[55] "From Somalia to Nigeria: Jihad," Katherine Zimmerman, *The Weekly Standard,* June 18, 2011. Available at: *http://www.weeklystandard.com/blogs/somalia-nigeria-jihad_574838.html.*
[56] "Nigeria's Boko Haram: Al-Qaeda's New Friend in Africa?" Karen Leigh, TIME Magazine. August 17, 2011. Available at: *http://www.time.com/time/world/article/0,8599,2091137,00.html.*
[57] Stewart, supra note 35.
[58] Stewart, supra note 35.
[59] "Nigeria says Boko Haram, al Qaeda link behind U.N. attack," Camillus Eboh, *Reuters,* August 31, 2011. Available at: *http://www.reuters.com/article/2011/08/31/us-nigeria-bomb-investigationidUSTRE77U3BM20110831.*

tacts, and small transfers of money. It seems that some members of Boko Haram and al Shabaab were trained by AQIM."[60] The increasing sophistication of the attacks seems to support Mr. de Kerchove's belief that Boko Haram militants have received training and weapons from AQIM. Moreover, purported leaders of the sect have publically praised Osama bin Laden and al-Qaeda. Some reports suggest the bombing may have been a message from Boko Haram to AQIM signaling its desire to cooperate in terrorist operations.[61]

Greater than the threat of any two of these groups collaborating would be the threat of all three collaborating together. AFRICOM Commander General Ham warned that while he doubts the ability of Boko Haram, AQIM, and al Shabaab to carry out attacks against the United States directly at the moment, he does not doubt their intent to do so. General Ham has warned about the potential for a transnational terrorist network to develop in Africa if the rising threat potential of these three groups is left unchecked:

> "Each of those three independently, I think, presents a significant threat not only in the nations in which they primarily operate but regionally and . . . to the United States. Those three organizations have very explicitly and publicly voiced an intent to target Westerners and the U.S. specifically. . . . If left unaddressed, then you could have a network that ranges from East Africa through the center and into the Sahel and Maghreb, and I think that would be very, very worrying."[62]

Recently, a statement from a purported spokesman for Boko Haram, Abul Qaqa, appeared to validate the concerns of General Ham and others. On November 24, 2011, Abul Qaqa admitted that the sect does receive assistance from al-Qaeda, presumably AQIM, stating: "It is true that we have links with al Qaeda. They assist us and we assist them."[63]

POTENTIAL FUTURE TARGETS: ENERGY AND AVIATION SECTOR

Nigeria has proven reserves of up to 36 billion barrels of oil, the 10th largest in the world.[64] It is the largest oil producer in Africa and the fourth-largest supplier of oil to the United States. As of August 2011, the United States was importing 854,000 barrels of oil per day from Nigeria.[65] In 2010, this amounted to 43 percent of Nigeria's total petroleum exports and 8 percent of total U.S. pe-

[60] "EU official warns of spreading al-Qaida offshoot," Jorge Benitez, NATO Source Alliance News Blog, The Atlantic Council, September 9, 2011. Available at: *http://www.acus.org/natosource/eu-official-warnsspreading-al-qaida-offshoot.*

[61] Leigh, supra note 56.

[62] "African Islamist group seen as U.S. threat—general," David Alexander, *Reuters,* September 15, 2011. Available at: *http://www.reuters.com/article/2011/09/15/us-usa-defense-africa-idUSTRE78E13920110915.*

[63] "Boko Haram claims al-Qaeda links," News24, November 24, 2011. Available at: *http://m.news24.com/news24/Africa/News/Boko-Haram-claims-al-Qaeda-links-20111124.*

[64] "Why Nigeria Matters," Dr. J. Peter Pham, New Atlanticist Blog, The Atlantic Council, April 4, 2011. Available at: *http://www.acus.org/new_atlanticist/why-nigeria-matters-0.*

[65] "Crude Oil and Total Petroleum Imports Top 15 Countries," U.S. Energy Information Administration, August 2011 data. Available at: *http://www.eia.gov/pub/oil_gas/petroleum/data_publications/company_level_imports/current/import.html.*

troleum imports.[66] Nigeria also exports a mostly sulfur-free sweet crude, which U.S. refineries prefer to the heavier oil imported from Persian Gulf and Caribbean sources.[67] As a member of the Organization of the Petroleum Exporting Countries (OPEC), Nigeria has proven that it can flex its economic muscle and impact global oil production. In short, disruptions to Nigerian oil production can impact domestic refining in the United States and affect global oil markets.

The Niger Delta, where most Nigerian oil production takes place, has a long history of instability and violence. Kidnappings, bombings, and attacks on oil facilities are routinely carried out by militant groups who feel disenfranchised and left out of the wealth that oil production generates. While these groups have been hesitant to inflict truly crippling damage against these facilities because they have some economic stake in them, Boko Haram, which is believed to have no financial interest in the plants, has no such reservations.[68] Niger Delta militants have in the past cut Nigerian oil production significantly through sustained attacks on oil facilities.

In May 2007, protestors from the Ogoni tribe in the Niger Delta overran an oil pipeline, cutting Nigerian oil production by 30 percent.[69] That same month, militants from the Movement for the Emancipation of the Niger Delta (MEND), bombed three pipelines, decreasing oil production by 100,000 barrels a day for the Italian oil company Eni. This disruption caused oil prices to rise by 71 cents a barrel in New York.[70] A well-coordinated attack by Boko Haram could result in far worse damage, completely cutting off Nigerian oil production in a worst-case scenario. If that occurred, 8 percent of U.S. oil imports would be cut off, which could result in a spike in oil prices worldwide and soaring domestic gas prices.

While Boko Haram is based in the north, recent reports indicate that Nigerian security services were searching for Boko Haram members who had allegedly infiltrated southern territory.[71] Niger Delta militants also released a statement warning Boko Haram against any incursions into the Delta territory, vowing to join with security forces to drive them out if necessary.[72] Given the vulnerability of Niger Delta oil facilities, and the potential powder keg of multiple militant factions squaring off against each other, Boko Haram's infiltration into this area should be closely monitored by the United States and allies.

As discussed previously, Boko Haram has already adopted many of al-Qaeda's targeting tactics. If Boko Haram continues this trend,

---

[66] U.S. Energy Information Administration Nigeria Analysis. Available at: *http://www.eia.gov/countries/cab.cfm?fips=NI.*

[67] Pham, supra note 64.

[68] In the past, Boko Haram has carried out armed bank robberies and has distributed whatever money it has stolen to the general population rather than keeping it. While Niger Delta militants may rely on the theft of oil for their primary means of financing, Boko Haram's financing comes from different sources and would be less inclined to be concerned with the affects of production being completely shut down.

[69] "Nigerian Oil Production Falls After a Pipeline Hub is Overrun," Lydia Polgreen, *The New York Times*, May 16, 2007. Available at: *http://www.nytimes.com/2007/05/16/business/worldbusiness/16oil.html.*

[70] Ibid.

[71] "Boko Haram in the Niger Delta," John Campbell, Africa in Transition blog, September 19, 2011. Available at: *http://blogs.cfr.org/campbell/2011/09/19/boko-haram-in-the-niger-delta/.*

[72] "Boko Haram: N-Delta militants volunteer to join forces with army," Emma Amaize, Sweet Crude Reports, September 20, 2011. Available at: *http://sweetcrudereports.com/2011/09/21/boko-haram-n-deltamilitants-volunteer-to-join-forces-with-army/.*

Nigerian oil facilities will be in thecrosshairs. In 2006, al-Qaeda struck the Abqaiq oil facility in eastern Saudi Arabia. Abqaiq is one of the largest oil fields in the world with a capacity of 7 million barrels per day.[73] According to open source intelligence, on February 24, 2006, two suicide bombers attempted to drive two cars loaded with explosives into the compound. This operation—and many others—mirror recently adopted Boko Haram tactics, including the use of suicide bombers and multiple VBIED attacks.[74]

In September 2011, threats made by Boko Haram to bomb Lagos Airport prompted security officials to search all vehicles approaching the airport, causing major disruptions.[75] Although aviation has not yet been a Boko Haram target, it is worth noting that Nigeria is a major destination for Western travelers. On August 26, 2000, the United States and Nigeria signed an open skies agreement to expand commercial aviation between them. This agreement established a direct flight from Lagos to John F. Kennedy International Airport in New York City, easing air travel to and from Nigeria[76] It is conceivable that Boko Haram may seek to take advantage of the tremendous volume of Western passenger traffic coming through Nigeria and the security vulnerabilities that volume creates.

Following the attempted Christmas Day attack in 2009, investigations revealed that four full-body scanners given to Nigeria by the United States in 2008 had gone unused; top officials were found to have been unaware of their placement in Nigeria's four main airports.[77] Nigerian airports began to use body scanners actively in 2010. The United States can assist Nigeria in improving security at its major airports through efforts such as providing full-body scanners and security training. U.S. Immigration and Customs Enforcement (ICE) and Customs and Border Patrol (CBP) can train Nigerian immigration officials in how to more effectively identify individuals who can pose a threat to homeland security, process and admit foreign travelers, and share passenger name record information (PNR) to prevent another incident similar to 2009.

VII. COMMUNICATIONS AND MEDIA

MARTYRDOM VIDEOS

On September 18, 2011, *BBC News* reported that Agence France Presse (AFP) news agency obtained two videos, each 25 minutes in length, of the Boko Haram U.N. bomber that had surfaced in Nigeria. Pictured holding an AK–47 rifle with two other people standing

---

[73] "The Impact of the Abqaiq Attack on Saudi Energy Security," Khalid R. Al-Rodhan, Center for Strategic and International Studies (CSIS), February 27, 2006, pg. 2. Available at: *http://csis.org/files/media/csis/pubs/060227_abqaiqattack.pdf.*
[74] Ibid.
[75] "Bomb scare disrupts Lagos airport road activities," Emmanuel Chidiogo, *DailyTimesNG,* September 24, 2011. Available at: *http://dailytimes.com.ng/article/bomb-scare-disrupt-lagos-airport-road-activities.*
[76] "Nigeria," Encyclopedia of the Nations. Available at: *http://www.nationsencyclopedia.com/economies/Africa/Nigeria.html.* The full text of the agreement, formally titled "Air Transport Agreement between the Government of the United States of America and the Government of the Federal Republic of Nigeria," can be accessed on the Department of State's website: *http://www.state.gov/e/eeb/rls/othr/ata/n/ni/114137.htm.*
[77] "U.S. scanners went unused at Nigeria airport," Associated Press, MSNBC, December 31, 2009. Available at: *http://www.msnbc.msn.com/id/34645445/ns/us_news-airliner_security/t/us-scanners-went-unused-nigeria-airport/#.TsQzi1ZBU8k.*

against a wall, the suicide bomber asked his family to understand his decision and explained that the bombing was designed to send a message to the "U.S. President and 'other infidels.'"[78] The man, whom an alleged Boko Haram spokesman identified as Mohammed Abul Barra from Maiduguri, also referred to the United Nations as a "forum for all global evil" and praised Osama bin Laden.[79]

A BBC correspondent, Jonah Fischer, based in Nigeria, wrote in a brief analysis that the existence of these videos signals an elevation in the sophistication of Boko Haram's methods of communication. "They show an organization which is far different from the local group fighting a tit-for-tat battle with the army and police in northern Nigeria," said Fischer. "This is another indication that this is now another beast, more international in its ambitions."[80] The correspondent also suggested that the sophistication of the U.N. attack and the use of more advanced communication methods may signal the support of outside help.

INTERNET FORUMS

Even more indicative of the growing sophistication and threat potential of Boko Haram is the group's increased use of internet forums. In July 2010, the alleged leader of Boko Haram, Imam Abubakar Shekau, issued an online statement praising al-Qaeda in Iraq (AQI), and offered condolences for the recent killing of AQI members. In this statement, Shekau warned the United States, "Don't think jihad is over. Rather, jihad has just begun. O America, die with your fury."[81] This statement coincided with an online presence the group developed in 2010.

According to a September 28, 2011 report published by the SITE Intelligence Group, Boko Haram had developed an increased online presence that "seems to have contributed to the rapid increase in their strength."[82] According to the report, a representative of Boko Haram who went by the name "Abu Sabaya" began posting requests for help on the prominent jihadi forum Ansar al-Mijahideen English Forum (AMEF) in March 2010. He has solicited advice on fundraising and Arabic translation programs and has sought information on how to hinder the operations of security services monitoring the sect.

The forums have provided fertile ground for raising interest in Boko Haram's cause, and providing possible fundraising and recruitment opportunities. One member, "Aydan," predicted that Nigeria would become a new front in the global jihad, writing, "I guess a new front is about to open."[83] Abu Sabaya continued to post calls for help with the development of Boko Haram. In one post, he described the sect's efforts to build its propaganda and media capacity, stating: "As for the media productions . . . we are

---

[78] BBC News, supra note 1.
[79] Ibid.
[80] "Analysis—Nigeria UN bomb: Video of 'Boko Haram' bomber released," Jonah Fisher, BBC News, September 18, 2011. Available at: *http://www.bbc.co.uk/news/world-africa-14964554.*
[81] "Suicide bomber hits UN office in Nigerian capital," Bill Roggio, *The Long War Journal,* August 26, 2011. Available at: *http://www.longwarjournal.org/archives/2011/11/boko_haram_kills_sco.php.*
[82] "Boko Haram Representative Solicits Guidance and Assistance on Jihadist Forums," Rita Katz and Margaret Foster, SITE Intelligence Group, September 28, 2011, pg 1.
[83] Ibid., 2 & 3.

rigorously working on them . . . we lack vibrant media experts in video production."[84] AMEF member Abu Hafs al-Gharib replied, suggesting that Boko Haram build links with an official jihadi media center, such as the Global Islamic Media Front (GIMF) or the al-Fajr Media Center. Linking with one or both of these centers would provide Boko Haram with much needed technical assistance and would also increase its legitimacy among the jihadi community. Linking with the official media centers was also the strategy al Shabaab adopted before it became a mainstream terror organization. In other posts written on 6 October and 27 October, Abu Sabaya requested fundraising advice and sought guidance on enhancing organizational structure and management.

Encouraged by Abu Sabaya's posts, other AMEF members began calling for jihad in Nigeria. In response to one post, a member who goes by "TheRealTruth" stressed the need for fighters to travel to Nigeria now, because security services have not yet been effective in securing borders, writing: "Sounds like a call! Where are the jealous sons of Islam to answer it! Right now its east [sic] to go to Nigeria, but may not be in the future . . . and another opportunity may slip us by!"[85] Echoing warnings by General Ham, forum member Abu Hafs al-Gharib responded by outlining a regional insurgency, stating: "Inshallah (Allah willing), Mujahideen from West Africa would be join with the brothers in Nigeria . . . jihad [will] spread out from North Africa, East Africa, West Africa and soon Central Africa . . . ".[86]

Not only is Boko Haram soliciting advice from AMEF members, but its posts appear to verify growing links between the sect and AQIM. One member, "Ansar AQIM," is an administrator and highly-regarded member of the forum. His posting history indicates that he has ties to AQIM. In an October 2010 post, he described links between Boko Haram and AQIM, claiming that AQIM commanders had arrived in Nigeria to train Boko Haram fighters. His full post read:

> "The assistance from the commanders of Al-Qaida in the Islamic Maghreb has reached Nigeria. I can't give any numbers of how many brothers from the Sahel region moved back to Nigeria to train the youth of the tawheed."[87]

According to the report, Abu Sabaya's updates during the spring and summer of 2011 "described a much-emboldened group."[88] On July 25, 2011, he announced in a post that the sect had successfully recruited defectors from the Nigerian security forces after they were sent to subdue Boko Haram fighters. The frequency of Abu Sabaya's statements also increased, as he began to claim responsibility for attacks, showcasing the sect's increased activity and capabilities during the summer of 2011.

---

[84] Ibid., 4.
[85] Ibid., 5.
[86] Ibid.
[87] Ibid., 6.
[88] Ibid.

VIII. OPTIONS FOR U.S. ENGAGEMENT

The rise of the potential threat of Boko Haram poses a new challenge to United States interests in a region where significant threats to U.S. National security already exist. However, the United States has also been presented with a unique window of opportunity. If the United States acts quickly on the military, intelligence, and diplomatic fronts, it can ensure the relative protection of U.S. interests while assisting the Nigerian government in containing Boko Haram.

Nigeria has a population of over 150 million people, making it Africa's most populous country. Nigeria also enjoys the continent's second-largest economy and has become a major regional player since transitioning from military to democratic rule in 1999. Nigeria's contributions to regional stability have not gone unnoticed in the United States. Speaking at an event in October 2011, General Ham noted, "Nigeria is the leading country for most activities in West Africa, in the Gulf of Guinea. They lead a number of other missions in a variety of places."[89] Nigeria's capital, Abuja, has played a major role in resolving regional disputes. It is the fourth-largest troop contributor to U.N. peacekeeping missions in the world.[90]

Unfortunately, the deteriorating security situation in Nigeria is a cause for concern, especially as Boko Haram's attacks become more sophisticated, coordinated, and deadly. Boko Haram and other terrorist groups such as AQIM—which is looking to expand its reach across Africa—would likely feel encouraged to exploit a destabilized Nigeria. Moreover, further instability could force Nigeria to pull out of various peacekeeping missions in order to increase manpower at home. If Nigeria were to collapse and become a failed state or descend into civil war, it could have negative implications for the United States and its allies.

In short, the rising threat of Boko Haram presents the United States with an opportunity to expand diplomatic and military engagement with both Abuja and Nigerian Muslims in the north.

MILITARY AND INTELLIGENCE SUPPORT

U.S. security assistance to Nigeria was suspended briefly from 2003–2006 while the State Department restarted its International Military Education and Training Program.[91] Since then, U.S. security assistance to Nigeria has steadily increased. According to General Ham, the U.S. military currently enjoys "a very longstanding, and very helpful, very useful naval and air military relationship [with Nigeria]."[92] In 2007, the U.S. Navy started the African Partnership Station as part of a larger effort to enhance security in the Gulf of Guinea. This program has included visits to Nigerian ports and regional naval exercises with Nigerian and European counterparts. The United States also provides military training with an

---

[89] "General Carter F. Ham, Commander, U.S. Africa Command," Center for Strategic and International Studies Military Strategy Forum, October 4, 2011. Available at: *http://csis.org/ event/military-strategy-forum-general-carter-f-ham-commander-us-africa-command.*

[90] "Nigeria: Elections and Issues for Congress," Lauren Ploch, Congressional Research Service, May 17, 2011, pg. 1. Available at: *http://assets.opencrs.com/rpts/RL33964_20110401.pdf.*

[91] Ploch, supra note 90, at 30.

[92] Center for Strategic and International Studies, supra note 89.

emphasis on respect for human rights and civilian authority. The State Department, which has also engaged Nigeria through its African Coastal and Border Security (ACBS) program, has focused its assistance on peacekeeping support, training, border and maritime security, and increasing military professionalization.[93]

Cooperation exists to a lesser extent between the U.S. and Nigerian armies. Nigeria is a participant in the National Guard State Partnership Program and coordinates activities specifically with the California National Guard. The Nigerian Army has also received counterterrorism funding from the Department of Defense: $2.2 million for the development of a counterterrorism infantry unit, and another $6.2 million designated to the tactical communications and interoperability within its counterterrorism unit.[94] General Ham has reported that cooperation between the two armies is steadily increasing and has noted that the U.S.-Nigerian military relationship is in part being shaped by the rise of Boko Haram:

> " . . . in my visit to Abuja I had a great meeting with the chief of the army staff following President Jonathan's visit here with President Obama. And I think, we're now starting to find ways in which we can cooperate more closely. Very clearly Boko Haram has altered that relationship somewhat. And so we're looking for ways in which we can help, ways that Nigeria would like us to give help in developing their counterterrorist capabilities . . . "[95]

General Ham proposed that the development of Nigeria's counterterrorism capabilities could include providing non-lethal equipment and training, and helping security forces to be more precise in their use of force.

Despite General Ham's positive reviews of U.S.-Nigerian military cooperation, Nigerian capacity to combat Boko Haram in the north is limited. According to sources following the attacks, soldiers deployed in northern Nigeria have been deserting due to a lack of pay. Morale has been reported to be generally low among security forces based in the north. Residents feel that the security situation will continue to deteriorate, in part due to the fact that senior commanders still do not appear to take the threat posed by Boko Haram seriously. The inability of the government to pay its soldiers and the lack of urgency among senior commanders regarding the increasingly violent attacks waged by Boko Haram underscore the challenges the Nigerian state faces in to confronting this problem.

It is critical that the United States work more closely with Nigerian security forces to develop greater domestic intelligence collection and sharing with the U.S. Intelligence Community. Military cooperation is vital to a successful counterterrorism strategy. A possible model includes Yemen, with whom the United States built an effective intelligence sharing partnership following the Christmas Day 2009 attempted attack to hunt suspected militants. While

---

[93] Ploch, supra note 90, at 30.
[94] Ibid., 31.
[95] Center for Strategic and International Studies, supra note 89.

this relationship continues to pose challenges, it has had notable success, highlighted by the killing of Anwar al-Awlaki.

In a recent display of growing international concern surrounding the rise of Boko Haram, France has offered military support to Nigeria. Meeting in Abuja with his Nigerian counterpart, Olugbenga Ashira, French Foreign Minister Alain Juppe stated: "We shall fight against this phenomenon. We are ready to share any information. We are ready to coordinate our intelligence services. We are ready also to give our help in training cooperation . . . France is directly concerned with the question of terrorism. It goes against our interest in the region and so we are in complete solidarity with the countries of the region around the sub Sahara and around the Sahel . . . "[96] Lieutenant General Azubuike Ihejirika, the Nigerian Army Chief of Staff, said that in addition to the United States and France, Pakistan and Britain have also offered to assist with counterterrorism training.[97]

DIPLOMATIC ENGAGEMENT

The United States has begun to engage Nigerian Muslims, primarily through two U.S. Agency for International Development (USAID) programs in the northern states of Bauchi and Sokoto.[98] Moreover, Nigeria serves as a minor partner in the Trans-Sahara Counterterrorism Partnership (TSCTP), a State Department initiative aimed at helping a number of African countries in the Trans-Sahara and Sahel regions combat terrorist organizations.[99]

Active public outreach to Nigerian Muslims plays a critical role in containing Boko Haram. Boko Haram has so far rejected negotiations with the Nigerian government, and has attacked and killed Muslim leaders who supported the election of President Jonathan. The United States has begun to take steps to promote government action on the numerous grievances that plague the north and hinder the prospect of talks between Boko Haram and the Nigerian government.

The United States is one of the largest providers of non-military aid to Nigeria.[100] In 2010, Abuja received roughly $614 million in aid from the United States. This aid is focused on programs in democratic governance, economic reform, security service reform and professionalization, and education and health care services. However, the majority of the aid goes to HIV/AIDS programs.[101] In 2010, the Obama Administration established the U.S.-Nigeria Bilateral Commission to encourage dialogue on issues ranging from security and energy to anti-corruption as requested by Congress in H.R. 2410, the Foreign Relations Authorization Act for Fiscal Year 2010 and 2011. The Commission is composed of four working groups that meet on a regular basis: Good Governance, Trans-

---

[96] "France to help Nigeria with Boko Haram militants," defenceWeb, November 14, 2011. Available at: *http://www.defenceweb.co.za/index.php?option=com content&view=article&id=-21097:france-to-helpnigeria-with-boko-haram-militants&catid=56:diplomacy-a-peace&-Itemid=-111.*

[97] Ibid.

[98] Ploch, supra note 90, at 30.

[99] "The Trans-Sahara Counterterrorism Partnership," U.S. Africa Command website, *http://www.africom.mil/tsctp.asp.* TSCTP partners include Algeria, Morocco, Tunisia, Chad, Mauritania, Niger, Nigeria, and Senegal.

[100] Ploch, supra note 90, at 29.

[101] Ibid.

parency and Integrity; Food Security and Agriculture; Energy and Investment; and Niger Delta and Security Cooperation.[102]

The United States has begun to publicly pressure the government to tackle corruption, encourage greater investment in the north, address poverty and joblessness, and promote government accountability and transparency. Recent statements by U.S. Ambassador to Nigeria Terence P. McCulley pressuring the government to address these problems are a significant starting point, and such pressure should continue. Additionally, a USAID program called Leadership, Empowerment, Advocacy, and Development (LEAD), is assisting northern governments build partnerships between state and local governments and the private sector. The goal of this program is to improve accountability, governance, and the delivery of essential services.[103] Former U.S. Ambassador to Nigeria, John Campbell, suggests the United States could also support efforts to "make modern education more palatable to an Islamic population."[104]

In addition to increasing government transparency and accountability, concerns regarding airport security, the economy, and education must also be addressed. The Nigerian government has taken steps to improve airport security after the attempted Christmas Day airline bombing over Detroit, but the government has been less effective in addressing the economic and educational issues that plague the north. In these areas, the United States has begun to implement programs to assist local and state governments.

Foreign Terrorist Organization (FTO) Designation

According to the U.S. State Department, "the Office of the Coordinator for Counterterrorism in the State Department (S/CT) continually monitors the activities of terrorist groups active around the world to identify potential targets for designation. When reviewing targets of specific groups, S/CT looks not only at the actual terrorist attacks that a group has carried out, but also at whether the group has engaged in planning and preparations for possible future acts of terrorism or retains the capability and intent to carry out such acts."[105]

The legal criteria for FTO designation includes the following:

1. It must be a foreign organization.
2. The organization must engage in terrorist activity, as defined in section 212(a)(3)(B) of the INA (8 U.S.C. § 1182(a)(3)(B)),* or terrorism, as defined in section 140(d)(2) of the Foreign Relations Authorization Act, Fiscal Years 1988 and 1989 (22 U.S.C. § 2656f(d)(2)),** or retain the capability and intent to engage in terrorist activity or terrorism.

---

[102] Ibid., 28.

[103] Ibid., 30.

[104] "To Battle Nigeria's Boko Haram, Put Down Your Guns," John Campbell, *Foreign Affairs*, September 9, 2011. Available at: *http://www.foreignaffairs.com/articles/68249/john-campbell/to-battle-nigerias-boko-haram-put-down-your-guns.*

[105] Complete information regarding legal criteria for FTO designation can be found at the website of the U.S. Department of State, Office of Coordinator for Counterterrorism. Available at: *http://www.state.gov/s/ct/rls/other/des/123085.htm.*

3. The organization's terrorist activity or terrorism must threaten the security of U.S. nationals or the national security (national defense, foreign relations, or the economic interests) of the United States.

Based on Boko Haram's evolution and recent public warnings by the U.S. State Department to U.S. citizens in Nigeria, Boko Haram may meet the legal criteria for State Department FTO designation.[106] Such designations are subject to a rigorous statutory process and through investigation, which the State Department needs to initiate. If Boko Haram were to be designated an FTO, it would support U.S. Intelligence Community efforts to curb the group's financing, stigmatize and isolate it internationally, heighten public awareness and knowledge, and signal to other governments the United States takes the threat from Boko Haram seriously.[107]

IX. CONCLUSION

Boko Haram's attacks are occurring at their greatest frequency since the sect emerged from hiding in 2010. The sophistication of its tactics, use of the internet, and its recent attack on the U.N. headquarters in Abuja all point to a dangerously evolving organization.

Debate exists regarding Boko Haram. Some believe it is little more than a grassroots insurrection with no defined leader or structure. Others believe that core Boko Haram, as it is understood, is a very small group of individuals who simply consider themselves to be the followers of their slain leader Mohammed Yusuf. Despite our lack of understanding of Boko Haram, the movement appears to have significant sympathy among many Nigerian Muslims. Coupled with the grievances that plague the north, the environment is ripe for recruitment. Recent evidence alludes to the sect's potential desire to join the ranks of international jihadist organizations. American, Nigerian, other African, and European officials have all expressed concern over the sect's communication with AQIM and al Shabaab. An alliance, or at the very least cooperation between the groups, can prove costly for the stability of Africa, the Sahel, and American interests.

Perhaps most striking is how little is known about Boko Haram. The sect remained relatively off the radar screen of the U.S. Intelligence Community until the U.N. headquarters attack, its first non-Nigerian, international target. Similar attacks have signaled the beginning of new phases for other extremist groups such as AQIM in the past.

The U.S. Intelligence Community has underestimated the threat potential of terrorist organizations in the recent past, most notably AQAP in Yemen and TTP, the Pakistani Taliban. Both of these groups were believed to be focusing on regional targets in the Arabian Peninsula and South Asia. The attempted bombing of a U.S. passenger jet over Detroit on Christmas Day 2009 by a Nigerian Muslim trained by AQAP, and the attempted bombing of New York's Times Square by a Pakistani American trained by TTP left

---

[106] "Emergency Message for American Citizens," United States Diplomatic Mission to Nigeria, November 5, 2011. Available at: *http://nigeria.usembassy.gov/emac_2011.html.*
[107] U.S. Department of State, supra note 105.

many in the Intelligence Community caught off guard. This report seeks to avoid another intelligence lapse by calling attention to the potential threat Boko Haram can pose to U.S. interests abroad and in the homeland. At this time, the risk of an attack by Boko Haram on the U.S. homeland may be low, but it is advisable to take the threat seriously and prepare accordingly.

○

CPSIA information can be obtained at www.ICGtesting.com
Printed in the USA
BVOW06s1023230714

360217BV00018B/397/P